"I HAVE TO WRITE IT DOWN" 30 DAYS OF WALKING IN PURPOSE

AUTHOR: SHONTORIAL P. GILBERT

Edited by Joshua Battle

Copyright ©2019 Shontorial P. Gilbert

No part of this book may be reproduced in any many written, electronic, recording or photocopying without written permission of the publisher or author.

All rights reserved.

1st Edition

ISBN: 9781795285353

Printed In U.S.A.

FOREWORD

By Joshua Battle

I am amazed by Shontorial Gilbert's book, I Have To Write It Down. It is one of the most encouraging books I have ever had the pleasure of reading. Not only is it filled with great scriptural and spiritual insight, but it is also saturated with personal words of encouragement and wisdom that will aid you on the journey to your destiny and the fulfillment of your God given purpose.

I have literally known Shontorial for her entire life and have watched her on many occasions have one conversation with an individual and was able to see the God given greatness within them, that even they themselves could not. Each chapter, every scripture, every exercise contained in I Have To Write It Down, will help the reader dig deeper not only into understanding their own thought processes, but as you meditate on the scriptures therein and complete the daily writing exercises, you will gain an insight into the mind, heart, and will of God for your life.

"I know what I'm doing. I have it all planned out—plans to take care of you, not abandon you, plans to give you the future you hope for." – Jeremiah 29:11 (THE MESSAGE BIBLE)

I HAVE TO WRITE IT DOWN helps you to realize some simple yet profound biblical truths. Everything that God made is good and very good. And that includes **YOU**. That includes every part of you. Even the way you think. Your ideas. Your Goals. Your aspirations. Your plans. God can use every part of you to bring greatness to the world because He created you to be great.

I HAVE TO WRITE IT DOWN helps to tear down the walls of fear, anxiety, rejection, even despair and depression that will prevent you realizing the greatness that is within you. *"For God hath not given us the spirit of fear; but of power, and of love, and of a sound mind."* – 2 Timothy 1:7

Shontorial has a unique approach and a prophetic insight that delves deeply into the crippling fears and anxieties that cause delay, stagnation, unproductivity, and even negativism in the life of the reader. In other words, those things that we allow within us to get in our own way or the things we do to "shoot our own selves in the foot" can and will be eradicated as you chart your thoughts through the God given wisdom contained within the chapters of I HAVE TO WRITE IT DOWN.

If you have found yourself in a stuck position, wondering how to move forward or simply where to begin, I HAVE TO WRITE IT DOWN will help you to "start to start". Shontorial's insight will help you to see that you don't have to reinvent the wheel or wait for the perfect time to see your God given vision come to pass. All you need to do is start right where you are, by writing the vision down and making it plain. (Habakkuk 2:2)

One of the most amazing things that you will quickly realize as you read and complete the daily writing challenges of this book is that God's plans for your life are much bigger than you could have ever imagined. In fact, you will undoubtedly discover that in order to be able to fully comprehend the magnitude of it all, you will quickly recognize that "I HAVE TO WRITE IT DOWN!!! "

Introduction

I will stand upon my watch, and set me upon a tower, and I will watch to see what he will say unto me, and what shall I answer when I am reproved. And the Lord answered me, and said, "Write the vision and make it plain upon tables, that he may run that readeth it. For the vision is for an appointed time, but at the end it shall speak and not lie: though it tarry wait for it; because it will surely come, it will not tarry."

-Habakkuk 2:1-3

This devotional Journal is the result of an inspiration by a Life Coach, who helped me to reinvent my thought process by encouraging me to put my thoughts on paper. I didn't realize the depth of confusion there was in my thought process. There were several things that I desired to do but did not know how or where to start. Cluttered ideas overshadowed my ability to clearly see the path God had set before me. It was during my second session with my Life Coach, that she suggested the idea of organizing my thoughts by putting them on paper.

Writing my ideas and vision down helped me to find and follow the set path to my purpose. It unfolded before because I was able to plainly see and read it. As I wrote, my thoughts became words, and my words became the manuscript for this book.

The title, *"I HAVE TO WRITE IT DOWN"* was birthed during my struggle and desire to get into the secret place of God and is founded based on Habakkuk 2:2, writing down the vision and making it plain. [*AND THE LORD ANSWERED ME, AND SAID, WRITE THE VISION, AND MAKE IT PLAIN UPON TABLES, THAT HE MAY RUN THAT READETH IT.* – HABAKKUK 2:2 KJV]

I was desperate to hear what God had to say to me directly, concerning His thoughts and plans for my life, and to clearly know my purpose, call and destiny. My desire at the time was to grow personally and professionally, but during the process, I discovered more about myself and who God created me to be. I hope this devotional journal inspires you to take a closer walk with God through communion with Him, as you seek His will for your life. This book is intended for people who feel stagnated or stuck in life or on the job. It is for people who lack direction and spiritual growth, or if you are in a dry place, seeking to find meaning and purpose to your life.

Although journaling will help you to discover areas in your life that needs transforming and organization, I cannot promise that you will be transformed overnight. But, my hope is that you will vividly see what is inside of your heart, mind, soul, and spirit. My deepest hope and prayer for you, is that you will see that your destiny will align with the purpose that God has created for you before the foundations of this world. I am excited about your journey, and I hope that you are too!

Day 1

WHAT ARE YOU CREATED TO DO? YOU WERE BORN WITH A PURPOSE!

Have you ever come to a point in your life where you knew that God had a plan and purpose, but you had yet to discover it? Maybe you have wondered why you encountered numerous setbacks or delays and did not think that you would ever finish what you had started. In your determination to find your true purpose and destiny, sometimes it may seem that you will never get there. Do not become discouraged. Life sometimes will take you around many loops and curves and the road map may lead to what seems to be a detour. Do not fret! Simply take the scenic route! In frustration, you may cry out that enough is enough and want to give up and throw in the towel! This is the perfect time to surrender your will to God. Allow Him to help you find your way to the path that will place you on the right road to finding purpose. No matter how large or small, remember you were created with a purpose!

Scripture Meditation: For I know the plans I have for you, declares the Lord, plans to prosper you and not to harm you, plans to give you a hope and a future. Jeremiah 29:11 (NIV).

Challenge: As you reflect on this devotion, ask yourself

these questions: What am I passionate about? What drives me? What was I born to do? What will it take for me to get there?

_____
_____
_____
_____
_____
_____
_____
_____
_____
_____
_____
_____
_____
_____
_____
_____
_____
_____
_____
_____
_____

Day 2

"Write The Vision"

Is your dream so large that you can't see how it is going to come to pass, or believe that it could ever happen, or could it be that you are going through a valley experience and you can't dream at all? Maybe your dream is too small, and God is pushing you to dream bigger. Sometimes, God will allow you to enter a place of discomfort, to cause you to stretch and grow. A perfect example is the eagle. The eagle will make the nest uncomfortable for her eaglets that they may learn how to soar. God has exactly what you need, and the plan to work it out. "Trust in the Lord with all thine heart and lean not into thine own understanding (Proverbs 3:5)." God will place you on the right path and put you on a divine collision course with destiny! "Do not despise the day of small beginnings" (Zechariah 4:10). Dreaming is only the first step to seeing your vision come to pass. Writing the vision is essential to materializing what you want. Continue to increase in faith, hold your plans up before God and watch Him provide the rest.

Scripture Meditation: *And the Lord answered me, and said, Write the vision, and make it plain upon tables, that he may run that readeth it.* Habakkuk 2:3 (KJV)

Challenge: Write down your vision! What drives me? What am I passionate about? What are the next steps to take for my vision to begin to manifest?

Reflection: Do you have the endurance to wait if the vision tarries, or will you be ready if the vision runs quickly at the appointed time?

Day 3

YOU HAVE TO GO THROUGH IT!

Have you ever wondered why it seems that one minute you are enjoying life, then the next minute, life starts happening? Through experiences I have learned that life is unpredictable! It will have its hurdles. This is the process that contributes to your growth and maturity. The process is often most uncomfortable, but necessary for your establishment. Maybe it seems that life was better when you lived as you pleased, unconcerned of the dangers, snares, hurts, and pains that may come. Maybe you are like Joseph, with an incredible gifting on your life that needs maturing. God allowed Joseph to experience different events, and even in the worst situations he found a way to trust God. One day Joseph found himself in a pit, sold into slavery by his own brothers, thrown into prison because of a lie, but eventually became second in charge only to the Pharaoh of Egypt. It was because of Joseph's faithfulness to God, that God used Joseph's gift to interpret Pharaoh's dream, which saved millions of lives including Joseph and his family. Despite all the bad situations that you may have gone through, God will use those bad situations eventually for your good! (Romans 8:28) Joseph's gift brought him before great men and so can yours!

Scripture Meditation: *As for you, you meant evil against me, but God meant it for good in order to bring about this present result, to preserve the many people alive. Genesis 50:25 (NASB)*

A man's gift makes room for him and bring him before great men. (Jubilee, 2000 Bible)

Challenge: Think about the hardships and trials that you have gone through. Reflect and write down how you perceive that God has used those trials for your good. Write down your gifts and talents. Reflect on ways you can use them.

_____
_____
_____
_____
_____
_____
_____
_____
_____
_____
_____
_____
_____
_____
_____
_____
_____
_____

_____
_____
_____

> "Despite all the bad situations that you may have gone through, God will use those bad situations eventually for your good! (Romans 8:28) Joseph's gift brought him before great men and so can yours!"

Day 4

FORGIVENESS

You may be wondering what forgiveness has to do with finding your path to destiny and purpose. On your journey to revelation in finding your path, know that forgiveness is essential. You must forgive others **and** yourself for past mistakes and mishaps, as well as those uncontrollable life circumstances that turned your world upside down. While in search of redefining who you are, and finding your purpose, look within your heart and reflect on the places you need to let go of, the people you need to forgive, and the offences you may need to be free of. What I have discovered during this process is that the more you hold on to things and people who have hurt you, the more you will hinder yourself from moving forward and being free. Internalizing hurts and pains lead to a thought process that is distorted. Bitterness, anger and rage will damage the soul and hinder the blessings God has for your life. Maybe you need to forgive someone today. Ask the Lord to search your heart.

Scripture Meditation: *Get rid of all bitterness, rage and anger, brawling and slander, along with every form of malice. Be kind and compassionate to one another, forgiving each other, just as in Christ God forgave you. Ephesians 4:31-32 (KJV)*

Challenge: What is holding you back? Write down the things in your heart that you need to release. Example: It could be family members, co-workers, past situations, etc ..

_____
_____
_____
_____
_____
_____
_____
_____
_____
_____
_____
_____
_____
_____
_____
_____
_____
_____
_____
_____
_____
_____
_____

Day 5

"REDEFINING YOURSELF IS A PROCESS"

Our growth cycle resembles that of flowers. We blossom in different seasons. There is a time when we will be radiant and beautiful, and that adds vibrant color to any garden. But there is also a time when flowers will look undesirable and begin to wither and die. With this analogy, I am not speaking of a final death, but the death that occurs when it is the season of a harsh cold winter. However, this season is necessary for the producing of beautiful blooms. In other words, when the natural process of nature has its' effect on creation, this type of death prepares the flower to live again and bloom beautifully, in its' proper season. You may wonder, what does this have to do with redefining yourself? You must understand that, there is a process. There is a time to be pruned, a time to die, and a time to live; Everything has its time and season, and it is made beautiful in its time.

Scripture Meditation: To everything there is a season, and a time to every purpose under the heaven. Ecclesiastes 3:1 (KJV).

And he shall be like a tree planted by the rivers of water, that bringeth forth his fruit in his season. Psalms 1:3 (KJV)

Challenge: Spend 5 to 10 minutes in quiet prayer and meditation. Seek the Lord concerning the season that you are currently in and what He will have you to do? How would He have you to go forward in this season? Write it down! What are some mindsets, attitudes or old ways of being that need to die in this season, so that you may blossom into who you were created to be?

_____
_____
_____
_____
_____
_____
_____
_____
_____
_____
_____
_____
_____
_____
_____
_____
_____
_____
_____
_____
_____
_____
_____
_____
_____
_____

Day 6

"Facing Your Fears"

I am reminded on numerous occasions why I shouldn't do this, or why I shouldn't do that, or why I shouldn't start my own business. How many times does your adversary tell you that you are not going to make it? Or that wholeness, prosperity, and wealth is not for you? Or you aren't good enough? The list of self-defeating mantras goes on and on. The minute you allow these thoughts to penetrate your mind, the more your adversary has a foot hold of fear implanted in your heart. Fear is crippling and debilitating. Most of the Israelites didn't make it into the Promised Land because of **fear, unbelief, murmuring** and **complaining**. These things will stop you from stepping out on faith and keep you worrying about matters that are not important. Don't allow your winning ideas and inventions to be buried because of fear gripping you and keeping you from launching forward by faith. Generations of exceptional gifts and creativity are hindered because of this stronghold. Begin to work your plans, materialize your ideas and watch how GOD will honor you. It is important to know that fear is not of God. He does not put fear into our spirits. You can overcome fear today with God's perfect love and gratitude.

Scripture Meditation: *For God hath not given us the spirit of fear; but of power, and of love, and a sound mind. 2 Timothy 1:7 (KJV)*

There is no fear in love. But perfect love drives out fear. 1 John 4:18 (KJV)

Challenge: Write down the fears that hinder you the most. What are some ways that you can overcome fear and unbelief? Use this scripture meditation to help you overcome fear by learning to trust your creator.

Day 7

No Matter What, Keep Pressing Forward!!!!

When you are on your way to greatness, adversities will rise against you. There will be times when you thought you almost made it, times when you were almost there, and times when you feel like you just don't have the energy to keep going forward. Ecclesiastes 9:11 reminds us that the race is not given to the swift, or the battle to the strong. The road less traveled is not often easy. It is a long daunting process, with dreams that are sometimes deferred. I have often visualized this road as a dirt road, with hills, bumps, curves, overgrown trees, and loneliness. Sometimes it seems that you are the only one traveling this road, but I stand firmly in encouraging you that you will get there! No matter what others may think, or how they may count you out. You may not get to your destination at the time that you planned, but just know that you will get there, and YES, it will be worth it in the end! When God births greatness out of you, the High Call is well worth it!

Scripture Meditation: *I press toward the mark of the High Call of God in Christ Jesus! Philippians 3:14 (KJV)*

Challenge: Think of the challenges that you have had to overcome so far to get where you are now. As you reflect on these challenges, write them down and remember to be thankful for how you have overcome them! As you write down each challenge, also write down at least 3 ways that you can continue to move forward.

_____
_____
_____
_____
_____
_____
_____
_____
_____
_____
_____
_____
_____
_____
_____
_____
_____
_____
_____
_____
_____
_____
_____
_____

Day 8

"IT'S NOT WHAT IT LOOKS LIKE"

It may look like your situation is never going to change, or that it is taking longer than expected to get to the place where you desire to be. I want to admonish you to continue to finish what you have started! "It's not what it looks like!" Your adversary would have you to think that your hopes and dreams are so far away, that you won't ever reach them. Or that you do not have what it takes to see your dreams fulfilled. Please be aware of the false images that play out in your mind. It's only an illusion. Whenever your adversary presents you with thoughts or images that are not true, maybe even emotions that play out as anxiety or depression; stand firmly and boldly by affirming what God says about who you are, and what your destiny is. Take these thoughts captive by affirming who you are in the Lord, and how God sees your destiny and your future! Indeed, He has a thought and plan for your life.

Scripture Meditation: *Casting down imaginations, and every high thing that exalteth itself against the knowledge of God and brining into captivity every thought to the obedience of Christ. 2 Corinthians 10:5 (KJV)*

Being confident of this very thing that he which hath begun a good work this in you will perform it until the day of Jesus Christ. Philippians 1:6 (KJV)

Challenge: For the next five days recite positive affirmations about yourself in the mirror, and what you will accomplish. Write down how powerful you felt each day after making these affirmations.

_____
_____
_____
_____
_____
_____
_____
_____
_____
_____
_____
_____
_____
_____
_____
_____
_____
_____
_____
_____
_____
_____
_____

Day 9

YOU ARE WORTHY: WHO TOLD YOU THAT YOU AREN'T GOOD ENOUGH?

Maybe you were the last one to be picked for the team growing up. Or maybe you were not the most popular in school. Maybe even your college professor or teacher looked you in the eyes and whispered to you, "You just aren't what I thought you would be." Whatever the situation might have been, contemplate on how these words penetrated your heart, played out in your mind, and how the feelings of worthlessness or rejection followed you throughout life. Do not become despondent in a season of rejection and denial, whether it is the denial of a loan, house, job, promotion, or even relationships. Although you may have learned how to cope and push past the hurt and pain of rejection, there is still a counterfeit voice that tells you: You are not good enough. The truth is; You are worthy! Maybe this is a clear sign that there is something greater than what you can see at the time. Instead of becoming despondent or wallowing in despair, defy what your adversary wants you to do by setting your hope and faith in God. Be affirmed of who you are in Christ. He knows your ending from your beginning. The very hairs on your head are numbered by the Lord!

Scripture Meditation: *But even the very hairs on your head are numbered. Fear not therefore: ye are of more value than many sparrows. Luke 12: 7 (KJV)*

Challenge: Journal 7 reasons why you are worthy and read them aloud! Begin your thoughts with "I am worthy because…."

_____
_____
_____
_____
_____
_____
_____
_____
_____
_____
_____
_____
_____
_____
_____
_____
_____
_____
_____
_____

Day 10

WHEN GREATNESS MEETS DESTINY

What will happen when destiny meets greatness? There is a champion inside of you! The Victory has already been won through Christ Jesus! Greatness does not develop overnight. True, greatness is innately in us through our Heavenly Father, but that greatness is lying dormant within you and is intended to meet up with destiny! Many times, you may search all around and try every trending fad that is popular, but greatness was placed in the core of your belly, waiting to be nurtured and discovered. Often you will not see it in yourself until God sends the appointed people in your path who see it in you, and at the appointed time will speak into your life. Look at Mary, Jesus' mother. God choose to use a common girl with a unique situation to impregnate with the greatest gift this world could ever receive. She was truly blessed and highly favored by the Lord and so are you (Luke 1:28)!

Scripture Meditation: *He that believeth on me as the scriptures has said, out of his belly shall flow rivers of living water. John 7: 38 (KJV)*

Challenge: Journal your thoughts: What will happen when greatness meets destiny?

Day 11

DON'T BE SURPRISED IF EVERYONE CAN'T SEE YOUR VISION

Don't become upset or discouraged if everyone cannot see where you are going. The truth is, it doesn't matter if others do not understand you: what is most important is that you are focused on the vision. You must become excited about your own. Many times, when your vision is large, others are thinking too small. The most important aspect is not to lose sight of where you are going. You have worked too hard to get to where you are, you have been through too much to turn around. I am reminded how on many occasions the scribes, Pharisees, and naysayers mocked Jesus and in other occasions people would say, isn't He the son of a carpenter, or that's just Mary's boy. They didn't know that the greatest man history will ever know came out of Nazareth. Just know that your vision begins from a seed that is planted; it will grow if you nurture it and nourish it in the right environment. Sometimes, this means changing your surroundings, or your perception and learning how to remain silent until your dreams begin to manifest.

Scripture Meditation: He said, "Leave, for the girl has not died, she is asleep" And they began laughing at Him. Mathew 9:24 (KJV)

Scripture Meditation: Let your eyes look directly forward, and your gaze be straight before you. Proverbs 4:25 (ESV)

Challenge: Reflect on the vision you have written…Seek clarity from God. Start making strides towards materializing your vision one step at a time.

_____
_____
_____
_____
_____
_____
_____
_____
_____
_____
_____
_____
_____
_____
_____
_____
_____
_____
_____
_____
_____
_____

Day 12

WHAT HAPPENS WHEN YOUR GROWTH SHIFTS YOU INTO THE NEXT LEVEL?

What happens when your level of thinking or your old way of being shifts into the next level, while you are still in an old place, surrounded by old people? Your old place can represent your job, relationships, patterns, or thought processes. Be aware that in your pursuit to find purpose and growth, the people around you do not necessarily change, unless God elicits the change. If you are not aware of this, you will quickly become discouraged trying to maneuver in your old environment. Be patient until God moves you or elevates you. Do not relapse or slip back into your old way of thinking. Be grateful for the opportunity to coach others along, if they are willing to accept you. Instead of boasting about your transformation and allowing pride to set in, be willing to demonstrate your growth through your actions, humility and character. Remember not to conform to the old patterns of thinking, but continually be transformed through the renewing of your mind. In the proper season, watch God move you into your wealthy place of purpose and destiny.

Scripture Meditation: Do not conform to the pattern of this world but be transformed by the renewing of your mind. Then you will be able to test and approve what God's will is—His good, pleasing and perfect will. Romans 12:2 (KJV)

Challenge: Reflect on how God has renewed (changed) your mind. Write it down! How can you be light in a dark place? Humbly demonstrate your light or change so that God will exalt you in due time and so that others may see Christ in you.

_____
_____
_____
_____
_____
_____
_____
_____
_____
_____
_____
_____
_____
_____
_____
_____
_____
_____
_____
_____
_____
_____
_____

Day 13

Hold Your Plans Up Before God

No matter how major, how minor, or how near or far, you must hold your plans up before God! When you are constantly searching your heart, seek the Lord concerning your paths and purposes, it is important to whisper them to your creator. He knows all about your plans and intentions even before you ask. He is the one who placed them there. "For I know the thoughts and plans I have towards you, says the Lord." Yet, He is waiting for you to discover this secret passion or desire, that you know not of. Sometimes you will think with a one-track mind concerning your plans, but God has placed many gifts and talents inside of you. Someone has need of what you have and at the right place and time, He will place you on a collision course with destiny. It doesn't matter who around you have the same business, or if someone else is already doing what you desire to do. Remember this: God chose YOU! You have a unique gift, and He will develop that gift while you are holding up your plans and thoughts before Him!

Scripture Meditation: *Open up before God, keep nothing back: He'll do whatever needs to be done: He'll validate your life in the clear light of day and stamp you with approval at high noon. Psalm 3:5-6 (MSG)*

Each of you should use whatever gift you have received to serve others, as faithful stewards of God's grace and in its various forms. 1 Peter 4:10

Challenge: Write down your gifts! How is the Lord calling you to use these gifts? Seek the Lord on how He desires you to use these gifts to bring Him Glory!

_____
_____
_____
_____
_____
_____
_____
_____
_____
_____
_____
_____
_____
_____
_____
_____
_____
_____
_____
_____
_____
_____
_____
_____

Day 14

TO WHOM MUCH IS GIVEN, MUCH IS REQUIRED: ARE YOU READY FOR THE RESPONSIBILITY?

Many times, when you are operating in your gifts before they have come to their fullness, there is an urge to move into your call before time. However, take time to realize and appreciate that God is grooming and polishing you. He must refine you in order that He can get the glory out of your life. Walking into your call prematurely can be dangerous for you and others involved. The refining process is to make you. God knows you far greater than you could ever know yourself. Before the greater arrives or before the promotion comes, He presses the impurities out of us, building character and working on our attitudes. Do not get discouraged or despondent when your promise (call, purpose or destiny) seems to be delayed. Instead, thank God that He is yet at work within you, preparing you for the greater gifts, greater anointing, and greater mantles that you will carry.

Scripture Meditation: *"For unto whomsoever much is given of him, of him much shall be required." Luke 12: 48 (KJV)*

Challenge: Be thankful that God looks out for our good! Reflect on how God has matured you. Write it Down! What have you learned from this?

Day 15

FINDING YOUR NICHE

What makes you authentic? There are many people with talents, gifts, and abilities that God has given them. Have you found your niche? What is it about you that draws people to you? How is it that two people can have the same job, the same title, ministry, position or business, but different people are drawn to one person or the other? They both can be equally great, but possess a different character, mannerisms, and dispositions. It is the anointing that God gives a person that draws people to the unique gift that you possess. Someone else may have the business that you desire, but God has designed you uniquely to supply the needs and demands of others. When finding your niche, think about what makes you, you. What can you offer people that no one else has, but you? Maybe it's your integrity, your character, charisma, or your excellent ability to encourage and listen to others. Remember, you are uniquely YOU!

Scripture Meditation: *I praise you because I am fearfully and wonderfully made; your works are wonderful, I know that full well. Psalms 139:14 (NIV)*

For we are God's handiwork, created in Christ Jesus to do good works, which God prepared in advance for us to do. Ephesians 2:10 (KJV)

Challenge: Think about the things that you are exceptional in. What brings you joy? What are you most knowledgeable about? How can you use what you have written to support others? Remember to encourage others along the way!

Day 16

STAYING FOCUSED

With many distractions, it is easy to lose focus on what you are trying to achieve to get to the next level of your life. Your adversary and the demands of life will snatch your attention by seeking to keep you busy; physically and mentally. Sometimes you may have to battle doubt, fear, and false thoughts that are meant to sway you away from finding or pursuing your purpose. The most important goal is to remain aware of what you have achieved thus far and where you desire to be. God calls us higher! His desire is that we launch out into the deep that we may know the deep things of Him. Even in your time of rest, it is important to take time to sit quietly and listen. There in your quiet time can you find peace and birth new ideas, passions and answers to life's difficult questions. Also, this is your time to rejuvenate and be restored. Not only can you find answers, but the Holy Spirit will commune with you and speak to you through your inner being. Paul reminds us to be anxious for nothing, with thanksgiving, make your request known before God and the peace of God shall keep your hearts and mind through Christ Jesus (Philippians 4:8).

Scripture Meditation: *The spirit searches into all things, even the deep things of God. 1 Corinthians 2:10 (KJV)*

So let's keep focused on that goal, those of us who want everything God has for us. If any of you have something else in mind, something less than total commitment, God will clear your blurred vision -you'll see it yet! Now that we're on the right track, let's stay on it. Philippians 3:15-16 (MSG)

Challenge: Do not focus on distractions you cannot control. Instead of looking at the negatives, write down things that did go well and are working for you.

_____
_____
_____
_____
_____
_____
_____
_____
_____
_____
_____
_____
_____
_____
_____
_____
_____
_____
_____
_____
_____
_____
_____
_____
_____

Day 17

Gratitude: Learn How To Be Grateful

Paul stated that he learned how to be content in whatever situation he found himself in, whether he was in need, or whether he was full (Philippians 4:11). I have found in life that being grateful is one of the secrets to contentment. No matter what current status you may find yourself in, it is essential to give God thanks! Being grateful and showing gratitude towards God will set you up for God's loving kindness, and favor towards you. Gratitude allows God to know that you are open to receive His blessings that He is waiting to pour out on your life. A grateful heart extends true worship towards the creator, and once you find yourself in this place with Him; He opens His heart and reveals His thoughts, secrets and plans towards you. All things work together to reveal your path to destiny and purpose. Remember to practice gratitude even in trying situations. Gratitude exposes the secret place of God's heart.

Scripture Meditation: *In everything give thanks: for this is the will of God in Christ Jesus concerning you. 1 Thessalonians 5:18 (KJV)*

Challenge: Express gratitude. Write down and recite the things that you are grateful for.

Day 18

Resist The Temptation To Complain

In this world, you will have trouble; however, be reminded that in Christ, you can overcome this world. During adversities, hard trials, and tribulations, it is easy to tuck your tail and run. Don't allow the temptation to throw a pity party set in. Things will happen, and plans do not always fall the way we intend. If they did, would there be a need to depend on God? The Israelites wondered in the wilderness for 40 years because of their murmuring and complaining. An 11-day journey turned into 40 years because they tested God through their bitterness and complaining. Do not look back when God delivers you from bondage. It is easy to dwell in the past and say, I had it better when . . . Or to become bitter from the things that happened to you. God wants to take you into a new place of freedom and prosperity; your promised place of destiny and purpose! Do not focus on the things of old and forget about the miracles that He has done in your life. Although you may be experiencing a wilderness situation right now, thank God for every miracle that He has orchestrated in your life. When adversities come, it seems justifiable to complain in your misery, but instead look at the bigger picture to receive revelation from Him.

Scripture Meditation: *Remember not the former things, nor consider the things of old. Behold, I am doing a new thing;*

now it springs forth, do you not perceive it? I will make a way in the wilderness and rivers in the desert. Isiah 43: 18-19 (ESV)

Challenge: Release those things that are troublesome to you, whether it is your job, money, co-workers, friends, family and etc. Write them down and give them to God. Allow Him to free you from the bondage of murmuring and complaining.

_____
_____
_____
_____
_____
_____
_____
_____
_____
_____
_____
_____
_____
_____
_____
_____
_____
_____
_____
_____
_____
_____
_____
_____

Day 19

SUFFERING: WHY DO BAD THINGS HAPPEN TO GOOD PEOPLE?

Life is inevitable. It happens to the best of God's people. As long as there is sin, sickness, and evil in this fallen world, unfortunate events will happen. The encouragement in these situations is that God will never leave you, nor forsake you. His promise of divine protection will keep you in all of your ways when you abide under the shadow of the almighty (Psalms 91). Know that as His child, no one can pluck you out of His hands (John 10:28). God knows the very number of hairs on your head (Mathew 10). Furthermore, suffering produces growth and maturity in you. DO not be deceived by the enemy. God doesn't inflict pain on His people. He is a loving and gracious God, but just like He allowed Job to experience hardships and losses, He undoubtedly knew that Job would remain faithful and righteous before Him. After Job experienced this time of suffering, Job was given double for his trouble. You may wonder what does suffering have to do with destiny and purpose, but out of such pain, God can produce and birth goodness out of your life. These experiences can be used as a testimony to help others.

Scripture Meditation: *My suffering was good for me, for it taught me to pay attention to your decrees. Psalms 119: 71 (NLT)*

Challenge: What are some heartaches and pains that you have suffered? Meditate on how God has now worked these things for your good. If you are still in a place of suffering, meditate on the scripture verses referenced above so that you may find comfort.

_____
_____
_____
_____
_____
_____
_____
_____
_____
_____
_____
_____
_____
_____
_____
_____
_____
_____
_____
_____

Day 20

THE KEY TO TRUE HAPPINESS

I have found that life has many phases and different cycles. It almost compares to the different seasons; there is a spring, summer, winter, and fall. I am fully persuaded that in our human nature, no one is exempt from experiencing the winter season, which brings about sadness and maybe even a mild case of depression. What I am most assured of is that even when things are happening on the outside of you, you do not have to succumb to the emotional roller coaster. Only you are in control of your emotions and how well you respond to life's situations. Surely there are some things that will happen that can naturally cause grief and heartache, but there are minor things that happen, which should not have any power over your happiness, peace, or joy. You have the power to decree and declare a thing and it shall be established. Imagine what will happen when boldness comes into your spirit and you begin to decree and declare success and prosperity into your destiny and future! Picture how the original you, who God created you to be, will rejoice on the inside and awaken every fiber of greatness that is established on the inside of you!

Scripture Meditation: *Thou shall also decree a thing, and it shall be established unto thee: Job 22:28 (KJV)*

For we do not have a high priest who is unable to sympathize with our weaknesses, but one who in every respect has been tempted as we are, yet without sin. Hebrews 4:15 (ESV)

Challenge: Practice being present. Resist the temptation to dwell on the past and jump into the future. Just try to enjoy where you are presently. If you are not where you desire to be at the moment, that's okay too. Just remember to experience where you are currently.

Day 21

Speak Life Into Existence

On your way to destiny and greatness, speaking life into existence takes intentional meditation and practice. I am reminded of how Proverbs admonishes us that as a man thinks in his heart, so is he. Although your current status may not be where you desire it to be, it is important to call those things that be not as though they were (Romans 4:17). One concept that I have learned is that your thought process will dictate how you feel, as well as your actions and your responses to situations. God desires for all of us to "prosper and to be in health even as our soul shall prosper" (3 John 1:2). Yes, that means that prosperity is in our destiny and it is for the believer! Trust God to work miracles and favor in your life! You will be surprised how trusting in your creator to provide, will produce Great and Mighty outcomes! God is a loving God, an awesome and mighty God! His desire is not to see His people in lack. I am not only referring to resources and finances, but also spiritually, health, and emotionally. Start today by calling your purpose and destiny into divine alignment with God's will and purpose for your life!

Scripture Meditation: *Death and life are in the power of the tongue: and they that love it shall eat the fruit thereof. Proverbs 18:21 (KJV)*

Challenge: Begin to speak those things that you desire into the atmosphere! Do this as often as possible. Write them down and check those things off once they begin to come to pass!

_____
_____
_____
_____
_____
_____
_____
_____
_____
_____
_____
_____
_____
_____
_____
_____
_____
_____
_____
_____
_____
_____

Day 22

STEPPING INTO YOUR DESTINY

It wasn't by chance the series of events that took place in your life led you down the path of your destiny. Whether the events were good or bad, it was not by happenstance! Everything and all things work together for our good. You may have had to shed many tears, or suffer heartaches behind the situation, but experience will teach life lessons. Your experiences can push you to the next level you need to be concerning your future. It could have been that dead in job that caused you so much frustration, or haters on your job that persecuted you. There are some things in life I wish I could reverse, but in the end, I am grateful for the strength that I have gained, the wisdom that I have ascertained, passions that I have discovered, and the Glory that God has gotten out of my life. Don't look back in regret. SIMPLY STEP INTO YOUR DESTINY!!!!!

Scripture Meditation: *Jesus began to show his disciples that he must go to Jerusalem and suffer greatly from the elders, the chief priests, and the scribes, and be killed and on the third day be raised. (Matthew 16:21)*

Challenge: Keep looking ahead......Continue to make strides in moving forward (Whatever forward means for you).

Day 23

IN EVERYTHING YOU MUST HAVE BALANCE

In everything we should be mindful of the fruit of the Spirit: Self-Control and Temperance. Balance keeps us in a good place of stability. There are some things you will simply have no control over, but the things in which you do have control; using wisdom to find balance is the key. Balance is essential. Solomon reminds us that living loosely is vanity. If you are aspiring to go to the place that God is beckoning you to go, you must learn how to be a good steward of what you have right now! If you are unsure of what to do, ask God which way you should go and how you should oversee what He has given you: whether it is time, finances, family, spouse, gifts, talents, school, work, or time with Him. Self-Control will support you in having enough energy reserved when the time of opposition comes and when life demands more than you think you have to give. Remember that balance keeps you healthy!

Scripture Mediation: *But the fruit of the Spirit is love, joy, peace, forbearance, kindness, goodness, faithfulness, gentleness and self-control. Galatians 5:22-23 (NIV)*

Challenge: Sit down, reflect and weigh tasks, or things that are of a lesser priority; weed them out! Start by only focusing on things that you have control of and prioritizing what is most important. "Write them down!"

Day 24

THE CLOSER YOU GET TO YOUR DESTINY; THE MORE DISTRACTIONS WILL COME: DON'T LOSE HEART!

The closer you get to fulfilling God's assignment and purpose for your life, the more distractions will come and present themselves to you. These distractions are meant to shift you off course and send your mind back into the old way of thinking. Distractions are disruptions. You must know and recognize them when they come. Some are meant to sift you of your joy, throw you off course, and set you back from what God has called you to do. If you allow yourself to become distracted, it is easy to start majoring in the minors and placing all your focus and attention on things of little importance. Count it all joy when you fall into *diverse* temptations (James 1:2). Just know that the trying of your faith produces patience. The closer you are to assuredly know who God has predestined you to be, you can expect that distractions will follow. Just know that there is not a devil in hell that can stop you from what you have been commissioned to do! Some distractions may come in the form of trouble on the job, finances, and things going wrong that cause frustration, or persecutions, and many other forms of trouble that can cause hindrances.

Scripture Meditation: *My brethren, count is all joy when you fall into diverse temptations; Knowing that the trying of your faith worketh patience. James 1: 2-3 (KJV)*

Challenge: Whenever a distraction presents itself in the form of an adversity, do the opposite of what is expected! Keep pressing forward!

_____
_____
_____
_____
_____
_____
_____
_____
_____
_____
_____
_____
_____
_____
_____
_____
_____
_____
_____
_____
_____
_____
_____
_____

Day 25

THE BATTLE IS NOT YOURS: DON'T WASTE YOUR TIME FIGHTING

"For the battle is not yours," says the Lord! You don't have to waste your time and energy praying about battles that do not belong to you. Some battles are too large for you and are sent to distract you. Oftentimes we fight battles that God has already given us the victory in. The only thing that needs to be done is to praise God for the triumph and enjoy the spoils that He has allowed you to recover from the enemy. When you sit back and allow God to fight your battles, He will give you peace over all the land. Do not deplete your energy by using it in the wrong places. Reserve your energy to listen and place your focus on matters that are most important.

Scripture Meditation: *Be not afraid nor dismayed by reason of this great multitude; for the battle is not yours, but God's. 2 Chronicles 20:15 (KJV)*

Challenge: Learn to let go! Make your request before God and take your hands off things that are not a necessity. What unnecessary battles are you fighting today?

Day 26

No Matter What Is Going On Around You: Look Within To Find Peace

As soon as your feet hit the floor in the mornings, center yourself to find peace. This is the kind of peace that man can't give and you can't get it from the universe; but only through God. When you are surrounded by quietness first thing in the morning, give God thanks for the peace that He has given you. Turn your mind off to the desire to jump head first into the day. The world did not give you peace and neither can it take it away (John 14:27). Your adversary will seek to throw many distractions your way, whether it is on the job, simply getting ready to go about your day, finances, or via news and social media, but God has given us a place that we can seek Him. I am reminded of God's promised protection; "A Thousand may fall to your right, and Ten Thousand to your left, but it will not come near your dwelling (Psalms 91)". Do not cave to the temptation to become disrupted by chaos. Know that Jesus is your Rock and your Salvation!

Scripture Meditation: *A thousand may fall at your side, ten thousand at your right hand, but it will not come near you. Psalms 91:7 (KJV)*

Challenge: Find time to make centering your thoughts on Christ the first thing you do when your feet hit the floor. Reframe from news and social media. Learn to take deep breathes in and out. Take note of how you can calmly handle the demands of the day!

Day 27

WALK INTO YOUR SEASON

At this point, you have survived many ups, downs, trials, emotions, and heartbreaks. But look at you now! Look at the place God has brought you to. Reflect on how God has fashioned you, how you have become strengthened and how your experiences have contributed to your growth. Out of every struggle came greater Glory! Now you are ready to begin walking in the purpose that God has pre-determined for you before the foundations of this world. Your experiences were not meant to hurt you, but to cause you to mature and grow. You have become like a tree, planted by the rivers of living water that will yield its fruit in due season, your leaves will not wither (Psalms 1). Grace has been granted unto you and God's goodness and mercy have followed you. Magnify your creator and thank Him for every lesson He has gracefully taught you. Now walk into your season!

Scripture Meditation: *And he shall be like a tree planted by the rivers of living water, that bringeth forth his fruit in his season, his leaf shall not whither, and whatsoever he doeth shall prosper. Pslams 1:3 (KJV)*

Challenge: Write down areas that you have matured or mastered. Next, write down the areas where there are still opportunities for improvement, or that you desire to grow in. Do not get discouraged, we are all still on the Potter's wheel!

Day 28

THE FATHER'S LOVE TOWARDS YOU: YOU ARE CALLED BLESSED!

Now that you are beginning to see your True Father, and your Creator's love towards you, your faith has strengthened and grown just a little bit more. Your faith has soared a little bit higher. You can do anything with the Father's love towards you: Nothing is impossible! Your creativity is flowing from the streams of living water from your belly. The Father's love towards you is blessing your endeavors, blessing your new journey, even revealing and blessing your destiny and purpose. His love has become oh so overwhelming to you! You can now begin to see the hand of God has been on your life this entire time. His love towards you is oh so amazing!

Scripture Meditation: *"But God demonstrates His own love towards us, in that while we were yet sinners, Christ died for us. Romans 5:8 (NASB)*

Challenge: Rest in the love of God and in His Presence!

Day 29

Your Experiences Have Shaped You

You have been on the potter's wheel the entire time. The Potter has shaped and molded you until He was well pleased with His design. The entire time that you have been on the potter's wheel did not feel good, you may have wondered why you had to go through this or that. Maybe you faced one thing after the other. You have wondered why it took so long to accomplish the goals that you have set out to do. Let me remind you that you were crafted to endure the experiences you have encountered, and you were fashioned to be more beautiful through what you have learned from your experiences. Now that you are beautifully and intricately molded, watch your creator get the Glory out of your life! You are ready for destiny and purpose to meet you!

Scripture Meditation: *"Like clay in the hand of the potter, so are you in my hand, Israel." Jeremiah 18:5 (NIV)*

Challenge: Create a quick summary of your experiences, and reflect on how God has positioned you to build your character and has gotten the Glory out of your life. Use these experiences as a testimony to help others.

Now, watch how you will find such meaning and purpose out of your life experiences, no matter how big or small.

Day 30

Tapping Into Your Gifts & Potential

You have yet to discover the fullness of untapped potential that is inside of you. Your 30-day journey is just a portion of what is to come! Whatever you find your hands to do, joyfully do it with all of your might, and watch how the Lord will bless you. Remember that your work is seen in the eye sight of your creator, and that your promotion is judged by Him. All the hidden talent and creative abilities that lay dormant within you, are just waiting to be used. Do not look down on yourself in doubt and disbelief about what you think you can't do. Look up to the Lord and tell Him thank you that His strength is made perfect in your weakness. The key to unlocking untapped gifts and potential is deep inside of you. From your belly shall flow rivers of living water. Remember, you are uniquely you!

Scripture: *Whatever you do, work at it with all your heart, as working for the Lord, not for human masters. Colossians 3:23 (NIV)*

For promotion cometh neither from the east, nor west, nor from the south. But God is the judge: he putteth down one, and set up another. Psalms 75:6-7 (KJV)

Challenge: Find Inspiration from Journaling and using the wisdom and principles of scripture no matter where you are in your spiritual walk with God.

Congratulations on beginning your journey to walking in purpose! If you enjoyed what you have read, and you desire to learn more about purpose. Please visit **www.wipurpose.com**.

Made in the
USA
Columbia, SC